The Golden Era

The Early History of the Golden Retriever

Malcolm Morecroft

The Golden Era

First paperback edition printed 2020 in the United Kingdom

ISBN No. 978-1-910815-21-2 (softback)
ISBN No. 978-1-910815-22-9 (hardback)

A catalogue record for this book is available from the British Library.

Typesetting by L Guescini/Mystic Mouse Design
All photographs and images used in this book are copyright of their respective owners.

"This book is dedicated to Angel. Like all of the Golden's we have had in the past, she is full of fun, loving, and our best friend."

Acknowledgements

I am more than grateful to Sharon Lynn and Lorenzo Guescini for once again willingly giving their assistance with this book, the sequel to my first (From Yellow to Golden), on the history and progress of the Golden Retriever.

Without the people and organisations listed below it would not have been possible to share the information given in this book.

The Kennel Club, with special thanks to Ciara Farrell, Colin Sealy, Louisa Foster, Heidi Hudson and Marianne Walker.

The British Library.

National Library of Scotland.

Highland Life Archives, Inverness.

Muckross House Archives, Southern Ireland.

The Hon. Mrs Townsend.

Lord Ashtown (Roderick Trench).

Nicholas Kingsley.

Turtle Bunbury.

Peter Mills.

Eileen Casey.

Henry Vivian-Neal.

David Wimsett.

Rob Menter.

Lynn Kipps.

And to my beloved wife who has spent many hours searching through books and old newspapers to ensure that the information that has been included is accurate.

Contents

Introduction

THE FIRST BOOK that I wrote on the history of the Golden Retriever was centred on seven people who were all connected, either by family relatives or in their working occupations. When I researched these individuals, I was aware that in addition to this group that there were a growing number of people who were supporting the breed through shows and working events. Even in the early years this was only to be expected as the breed was increasing its appeal to dog lovers.

This book, The Golden Era, describes the lives of some of these people. Again, it covers the years from 1868 to 1920, with just a few references beyond the last date. Most of the people knew each other and no doubt welcomed meeting at shows and working events and exchanging views on the development of the breed. They would also welcome others who showed a genuine interest in the breed so that the Golden Retriever would gradually become more popular.

The people that I have included came from different backgrounds and those who love the breed to this day should be grateful for what they achieved, often during changing and turbulent times.

And the dogs? Not so much turbulent times but changing times. During 50+ years of their progress the breed would be referred to as, special yellow retrievers – yellow retrievers – red coated retrievers – Tweedmouth retrievers, mongrels (how dare they!!) – Russian retrievers and Golden retrievers. The last of these live on to this day - and will for many years to come.

If you have read the first book, From Yellow to Golden - The Stately Heritage of the Golden Retriever, you will notice it has been necessary to repeat some parts of it in the first chapter, in order to give context for those who don't yet have a copy.

If you would like to purchase a copy of either book, please see details at the end.

Writing both books has given me a lot of pleasure and I sincerely hope that you get a lot of pleasure from reading them too.

❧ 1 ❧

In The Beginning

ONE FINE DAY in the summer of 1864 a father and son were walking on the South Downs in Sussex taking a route very near to Stanmer Park. The Park, with its Georgian House, was the country estate of the 3rd Earl of Chichester, Henry Thomas Pelham. Father and son had a good deal to talk about. The son had just returned from his first full year at Harrow School and his father, who years before had also attended the same school, was not only eager to find out how his son's studies were progressing, but also wanted news of any of the tutors that may still have been at the school from his days. The son eagerly told his father about his studies - he did want to succeed in these - but as to the tutors that his father may have known, his conversation was not quite as enthusiastic. The son's main interest was to find out the latest news from his father's estate at Guisachan in Inverness-shire. Even in his informative years the son was looking forward to travelling to the estate to enjoy part, at least, of the shooting season.

Who were the Father and Son?

The Father was Dudley Coutts Marjoribanks who it is acknowledged by most people to have developed a breed of dog which we now know as the Golden Retriever, which after over 100 years is one of the most popular and well recognised of the canine world.

And the Son - Edward, not only followed his father through his schooling at Harrow, but in later years was to succeed him as Member of Parliament for Berwickshire. When his father passed away in 1894, he inherited the shooting estates and property at Guisachan and at Edington in Berwickshire, both of which had been looked after by the Marjoribanks family for a number of years.

During their walk the father and son had a chance encounter with a Shoemaker, which started a sequence of events that led to the origins of the Golden Retriever. The Shoemaker had a light-coloured dog with him which impressed Dudley and his son, to such an extent that they both wanted to know more about it. They were told that he obtained the dog (in fact, the only dog with a fair coat from a litter of black retrievers) in return for a debt due to him from a gamekeeper by the name of Obediah Miles, who worked on the Stanmer Estate and had been appointed by the Earl of Chichester in September 1857. It is assumed that this dog was the flat-coated retriever, as even today there are a few Golden Retrievers that have coats with single black hairs and some even carry a flash of black.

Dudley was impressed by the nature of the dog and offered to buy it from the Shoemaker. A deal was agreed but the Shoemaker would not accept money on a Sunday, so Dudley had to wait until the following day to finalise the deal.

Arrangements were soon made for the dog to be sent to his estate in Scotland. Which method of transport he chose is not known. Edward could have been given the task. A good opportunity for him to get to know his father's new addition and there would have been plenty of room in the kennels at Guisachan after Dudley had sold his 49 Greyhounds some years earlier for £836. In today's money this would have been over £36,000!

In whatever way Dudley's new acquisition travelled, it arrived safely. The gamekeepers were used to having dogs on the estate - the stud book, which Dudley kept for over 50 years, in 1866 lists 30 - but a dog like the one Dudley had purchased was more than likely to have generated some interest. Perhaps Dudley conveyed the message to his keepers that, *"in my wisdom I have bought this dog as a new addition to the kennels"*, to which one of the gamekeepers may have replied *"its name must be Nous"*, which happens to be Gaelic for wisdom. My view only, but you never know! What we do know is that Nous and its offspring would always be the first of Dudley's "special yellow retrievers" as referred to by Ishbel, Dudley's third daughter, on more than one occasion.

The characteristics that Nous showed in its early months at Guisachan must have given Dudley some ideas for mating his new arrival. We can never know exactly what Dudley hoped to achieve but he already had plenty of experience from the breeding of other dogs on his Highland estate and no doubt he would also listen to the views of the

Painting of Ada with the 5th Earl
this painting is in a private collection

In August 1872 the renowned Scottish artist Gourlay Steell visited Guisachan at the invite of Lord Tweedmouth, Dudley Coutts Marjoribanks. While there he painted this portrait of his daughter, the Hon. Mary Marjoribanks on her horse Sunflower. With them is one of the first Golden Retrievers, Cowslip.

Derivative reproduction copyright Lynn Kipps.

gamekeepers that he employed. From listening to them he would have had to make a reasoned decision as to which breed he hoped would be the best to repeat the characteristics that Nous showed. The dog that he chose was a Tweed Water Spaniel by the name of Belle. The owner of this dog was Dudley's cousin, David Robinson, who lived at Ladykirk House in Berwickshire, on the banks of the River Tweed - so a very appropriate name for a dog for this part of the country!

From the stud book, the mating was done in 1868 and the litter produced four puppies, that we know of, and they all had light coats - fair coats - yellow coats. Take your pick - they were what Dudley wanted - yellow being Dudley's preference. And he showed his preference not only by reminding his daughter that they were special, but also by the names listed in his stud book for 1869. Cowslip and Primrose were at Guisachan. Another, Crocus was not listed until 1870, with the added note - Edward's. Where Crocus was for this year we do not know, but it was obviously not with Edward as the previous year he was sent on his travels on what we now term 'the grand tour'. All the names denote they were yellow.

The fourth was Ada. By name the odd one? Not really. She was the first bitch that Dudley gave away, the first of the breed to leave Guisachan. The person who was entrusted with the fourth puppy was Dudley's nephew, Henry Edward Fox-Strangeways. He was the son of Dudley's elder sister Amelia. One assumes that Henry Edward chose the name but why Ada is not known. There is no one with this forename in the family line, not even second or third Christian name, and no one on the census returns over a twenty-year period named Ada - not even a favourite nanny!

The Marjoribanks and Fox-Strangeways families had been joined by marriage in 1844 when Dudley's elder sister, Amelia, married the Honourable John George Fox-Strangeways. Their only son, Henry Edward was born in 1847. When Dudley gave Ada to his nephew, he would have just celebrated his 21st birthday. And what a gift Ada would have been!

Ada left Guisachan within months of being born and went to live on the Melbury estate in Wiltshire. She was never included in the annual studbook that Dudley kept for more than 50 years but her name is mentioned in 1874 when she is listed as the dam (mother) to a retriever called Brass. Is it possible that John George returned his thanks to Dudley for giving him Ada?

I have no doubt that Dudley would have advised John George to keep a stud book or at least get one of his gamekeepers to keep one. If this was the case, then unfortunately it has not survived. What is known is that there was more than one gamekeeper on the estate, the longest serving of which was Sidney Hill who in 1891 was aged 44. His son Lewis aged 18 was also working on the estate as his assistant. At least four other gamekeepers were also employed, and others were at the Abbotsbury estate in West Dorset where the Ilchester family would entertain invited guests during the shooting season.

The two estates covered over 32,000 acres but with an unexpected turn of events a third estate was to come into the possession of the Ilchester family. It occurred following the death of Lady Holland in September 1889. She had lived at Holland House in London, since the death of her husband in Naples in 1859. When he died the barony became extinct. As there was no direct family to leave the property to, Lady Holland was left with the task as to who should inherit the property and the park. For many years it had been the focal point of those people regarded as being at the forefront of British society. These included literary, philosophical, and political luminaries of the time. Lady Holland eventually decided on what is called a reversion of lineage and prior to her death she arranged for the sale of the whole of the property to go to Lord Ilchester.

The connection with the late Baron Holland and Lord Ilchester goes back over 300 years - the first Baron Holland and the first Lord Ilchester were brothers! In her choice of leaving the estate to Lord Ilchester, Lady Holland was to prove that Sir Walter Scott's prediction that the estate would be sold off piecemeal for development, to be incorrect - at least in his lifetime. However, in another sixty years it would all change, and today very little that was the original house or grounds survive. Lady Holland died at Holland House, age 78 on the 23rd of September 1889.

The acquisition of this property meant that the Ilchester

family were now one of the largest landowners in the country. Melbury House with its extensive gardens and shooting grounds, was the family seat, while Abbotsbury was their holiday home, where family and invited guests would enjoy the shooting season. Holland House and the grounds would be used all year round. Many society events and dog shows were held here. The latter were a regular event, organised by the Countess of Ilchester, who was elected to the committee of the Ladies Kennel Association, founded in 1895. The following year the Countess opened the grounds for the second LKA show.

Dogs, both working and show, played a major part in the life of the Ilchester family. The working dogs were mostly kept at Melbury but there were also a number at Abbotsbury. Ada was at Melbury in her early days and spent some time at Abbotsbury. Holland House also had a number of dogs - full time. The Countess kept a few of her Yorkshire Terriers here and as a fascination for visiting guests two 'tan' retrievers named, Jupiter and Hector. True to the ways of retrievers, guests would remark about their gentle nature and kindly looks of friendship and their

The Countess of Ilchester

polite ways around the rooms of the grand house.

Without a surviving stud book, it cannot be proved that these dogs were not in the line of Ada, but with the description of their good manners around the house, it is not easy to discount this.

Henry Edward Fox-Strangeways, the 5th Earl of Ilchester did not forget Ada either. When she died in 1882 the Earl had a headstone erected to her in her memory at Abbotsbury - her country home, or her retirement home? Whichever, with the love of dogs that the Ilchester family had, Ada had a wonderful life during her 14 years - and was a special retriever!

It has been claimed by the Ilchester family on more than one occasion that other than Ada, Dudley kept all the bitches from the litters born at Guisachan. With due respect to the Ilchester family, it is somewhat difficult to agree with this. If this was the case, then the breed would not have progressed beyond Dudley's kennels. This may have possibly been 1868 to 1884, during which time the breed was nowhere near being recognised in the dog world. Dudley's reason for not giving any away, outside of the family circle, may have been that although they were, as his daughter Ishbel always said, her father's "special yellow

Ada's Headstone

retrievers", that he wanted to withhold them for a time to find out from his stalkers and gamekeepers on his estate how they were developing as a working asset.

This theory has some foundation as in 1881 Dudley's stud book has entries under retrievers for "Minor - sire Sambo (H.Meux) dam Topsy, pupped 1877, with Duncan" (which was no doubt Duncan MacLennan the head keeper) and "Sweep - bred by Lord Ilchester" - followed by what looks like "Crocus breed", with no pupped date for this entry, with McDonald - another of the Guisachan keepers. The doubt with this entry is that Crocus, by this time could have been retrieving in heaven! Or, that he was still up for the challenge! Two other points of note from this entry is that the sire for Minor was Sambo, "H.Meux" - and "Sweep" - bred by Lord Ilchester. Not much doubt that with names like Sambo and Sweep, they were flat coat black retrievers. This entry does show that these dogs were in the care and training of two of the keepers at this time and that Dudley would have been more than interested in how they developed and worked on the estate throughout the year and would also have been interested for the keepers to compare them with the yellow retrievers.

Minor and Sweep were recorded again in the stud book for 1882 and again they were with Duncan and McDonald but, for this year, there is a 'pupped' date given as 1880, so the keepers may also have been reporting to Dudley as to their progress with regard to the three year gap in their birth date. The entry for 1882 also clarifies the source of Sweep's breed line by stating "Bred by Lord Ilchester, Nous bred". So, not only was Crocus in heaven but Nous also - retrieving together? By 1882 there could well have been a second Nous. Throughout the 1880's the stud book did not record many retrievers. What it does show is that Dudley had used the Tweed Water Spaniel bred by his cousin and the flat coat retriever bred by his son-in-law in mating the dogs in order to see the merits of these for the future development of the breed.

It would have equated to a breed in its early years of development from one litter to the next. I do believe that he would have kept what he thought would be the best. To this day many breeders still do this, either for working or for show. Sometimes they are correct but at other times the runt of the litter turns out to win prizes time and time again. No doubt Dudley's instinct did not always come through as he hoped it would, even after taking advice from his keepers.

With the somewhat scanty evidence at the time as to the early development of the breed overall it does look as if Dudley was very much using his knowledge to bring about a valuable addition to the working breeds of dogs. It would take some time to achieve this.

IN THE STUD BOOK from 1870 to 1885 there appears to be no more than six litters, of which twelve puppies were entered in the stud book. It is almost certain that there were others.

So, what happened to them?

Where did all the dogs go?

✌ 2 ✌

The Early Pioneers

FROM THE EVIDENCE that we know of, it was in 1868 that the first yellow retriever left Guisachan, given as a gift to the nephew of Dudley Coutts Marjoribanks with no doubt some instructions as to its care.

This information is certain.

For the next two decades it is difficult to find reliable information as to where puppies from future litters would have gone, and they must have gone somewhere otherwise this new breed would not have developed and become as popular as it is today. When Dudley was away from Guisachan he would have wanted to be kept well informed of the development of the dogs and foremost in giving him this information would have been his head keeper,

A group of Guisachan Keepers and Stalkers in the Guisachan Tweed. The one with the telescope is Duncan MacLennan. Photograph kindly supplied by Mrs Joyce Stirling of Tomich.

Duncan MacLennan. He would have given his honest opinion based on the views of other keepers on the estate and in turn informed Dudley as to their progress. The picture shows some of the keepers. This was taken in the 1870's. Duncan MacLennan is shown with the telescope, in the centre crouching down. To the right is Alex MacGillivray, and behind them both is James Cowan, who, at this time, was the Kennelman. It has not been possible to put names to the others, or to the dogs, two of which are flat coats.

It should always be remembered that they were a new breed of retriever, and a working breed. Although the stud book often records that they were with Duncan, other keepers were no doubt entrusted with them, especially those who had worked on the estate for a number of years. We have an indication of whom some of them were, when, after the death of Dudley in 1894, and when his son Edward chose to sell the estate in June 1905, the prospective purchaser, Lord Portsmouth, instructed his solicitor to draw up an inventory of those who were employed. Information listed gives the accommodation that they had and how much they were paid. It contains interesting reading. For instance,

Duncan MacLennan, the Head Keeper who had worked on the estate for over 40 years, was paid £50.00 per annum, and was provided with one suit of clothes made from the Guisachan Tweed that Dudley had had designed for his keepers. He lived in a house, rent free, and was supplied with three ton of coal a year, and provided with two cows!

Duncan MacGillivray was paid £45.00 a year and was given one suit of clothes, again made from the Guisachan Tweed. He was single, age 24 and had a property provided rent free and described as *"a promising young man, steady and successful in work"*. Of all the estate workers he had a very good position as Head Kennel man, a position for which he had been well trained, as part of his time had been spent on the Edington estate in Berwickshire, under the excellent tutelage of Tom Walker. Duncan was the son of Alex MacGillivray who sadly took his own life in March 1905. Alex had been suffering from influenza for many months and chose to end his life by turning his rifle on himself. Duncan's remuneration may well have been based on his father's tragic death.

Another employee given rent free accommodation was

Donald Kennedy who had a property at Cougie, not far from the main house at Guisachan. All the keepers listed had their families living with them and I have no doubt that they would have enjoyed the long winter evenings around the fire - with a dog or two beside them. Some things never change!!

IT WAS ONLY THE KEEPERS who had worked on the estate for some time and had proved to be reliable and trusted members of the running of the estate, who were provided with accommodation. They were kept busy throughout the year but as the shooting season got closer other keepers were employed on a short-term basis. And there were plenty of them in the Guisachan area. However, some keepers (known as journeyman keepers) preferred to move around, going to an estate which was rented for the shooting season and which paid the most.

One of these was Kenneth M'Lennan who was born in 1839 at Glenelg. His father was employed as a fox hunter for an area which covered not only Glenelg, but also Knoydart and Kintail. In his late teens he often accompanied his father and the magic of the hills soon made a lasting impression on him. In 1870 he was offered a position as gamekeeper on the Fasnakyle estate to the east of Guisachan, an excellent opportunity for someone just 31 years of age. The estate had been rented for the shooting season by a Colonel Inge. His name was often entered on the visitors list at Guisachan during the shooting season. The following year he moved to Gaick where the estate was owned by a Mr Littledale. But he was only here for one year as a move back to Colonel Inge occurred in 1872. On his own admission, it was the area around Fasnakyle which Kenneth enjoyed the most and the picture shows him with one of the first retrievers.

He is not wearing a suit of the Guisachan Tweed denoting that he was not working for Dudley, although no doubt Dudley knew him and regarded him as someone reliable

Kenneth M'Lennan

enough to work the new breed. After the death of Colonel Inge in 1877 Kenneth was employed by a Joseph Spender Clay, who he regarded as an excellent sportsman. This was at Gildermorie Forest in the county of Ross and Cromarty. When Mr Clay gave up the shooting at Gildermorie, he took the shooting at Cluanie forest, not far from Fasnakyle, and Kenneth went with him, but sadly Mr Clay died suddenly in 1882. At the request of Mr Clay's widow Kenneth stayed on until the end of the shooting season.

It is not possible to give an accurate date for the picture of Kenneth with a retriever - no problem with recognising the breed of dog - but I believe it could have been taken around 1875 at Fasnakyle. Kenneth would be approaching his fortieth birthday and has the look of a weather-beaten gamekeeper. And the dog? At this date possibly not from the first litter by Nous, but could be the second? And was it born at Guisachan? Possibly - but not certainly.

Kenneth was a true journeyman keeper. He was one of many, and if they were reliable and honest, they were never short of work, all year round. He would always have had a dog with him and when it was one of the new breeds of retrievers it would have been a great example to those who saw it being worked. Being away from home did not worry his family. He did find time for home life, being married to his wife Betsy in 1865, and having three children by 1881. His son, Murdoch, born in 1868, followed his father, taking up gamekeeping by 1891. The same year the census lists Kenneth as a retired gamekeeper but he was also a widower. When his wife died, and where, I have not been able to find out. Kenneth may have been retired in 1891 but ten years later he was still enjoying the outdoor life and the census shows his occupation as Deer Stalker, living at Dalbeg Cottage, Dalarossie, Inverness-shire. By 1901 he was 60. When he died, and where, I also do not know. Did he work other dogs - most certainly yes and I do not doubt they were still Goldens; such was the appeal of the breed.

Kenneth M'Lennan was a true journeyman keeper, but other keepers preferred a secure home and their family around them.

This was the case with John Chisholm.

DUDLEY'S STUD BOOK for 1868 has a note in the right-hand margin which states "Nous sent to Aultbeath with McMillan". The question comes to mind - Why? And why was McMillan entrusted with taking Nous to this location? Aultbeath was a small group of properties at the far end of Glen Affric, some miles from where the main house of Guisachan is situated. McMillan was not a gamekeeper but one of the few farmers in the area looking after 39 acres and who lived at the gatehouse at Guisachan. No doubt he was trusted by the Marjoribanks family, as was his sister, Margaret, who was on the census for 1881 as one of two women in charge of the main house at Guisachan, the other being Annie McDonell. Prior to this, Margaret had travelled to London and was on the 1871 census at Brook House, the London home of the Marjoribanks family.

Nous was only at Aultbeath for a short time, as in 1869 he was listed in the stud book for that year back at Guisachan and it is more than likely Nous had a good time. It would be some years in the future that would give confirmation of this! It would also give an indication of the progress of the breed.

Just as important as to what Nous was up to at this time is the fact that the gamekeeper living at Aultbeath Lodge was John Chisholm who was born in the parish of Kilmarock, north of Guisachan. By the early 1870's John was married to his wife, Ann, and had two children Catherine and Mary. By 1881 they added Ann and Jessie to the family. Changes were on the way for John and the family when they decided to move from Aultbeath two years later. For what reason it is not certain. It could have been that they were suffering from the harsh winters and the isolated location of this part of the estate or that he was aware that he would not gain promotion on the estate for many years. Or did Dudley recommend him for a position elsewhere?

Whatever the reason John took a position of Head Gamekeeper at Muckross House near Killarney in Southern Ireland and his wife and children went with him. Every good gamekeeper needs a reliable dog - or more - and from research on the estate it is likely that more than one of the yellow retrievers went with him. Was this the outcome of the visit made by Nous to Aultbeath years before?

At this time the Muckross estate was owned by Henry Arthur Herbert. The estate covered over 47,000 acres of mostly lush, and very green, Irish countryside. The highest parts of the estate reached just over 8,000 feet and there were extensive forests. The climate was very different, compared with Guisachan - plenty of rain coming in off the Atlantic making for a generally milder climate. A welcome change for his wife and family and no doubt for the dogs. But did the dogs have much to do?

Henry Arthur Herbert did not spend much time at his property. He was enthusiastic with regard to shooting, but there was a distinct lack of game to be shot and there was even less deer. Imagine the crisis when the shooting season was approaching, and the guests had all been invited. Henry had an answer to this and being a wealthy individual at this time he bought both game and deer onto the estate and some of the latter were shipped over from Guisachan. All that way just to end up on the wrong side of a bullet!

However, some of them must have survived as year on year the shooting in the season improved and it was John who was given the credit. He was also credited with the work that he carried out on the estate with the retrievers, as mentioned in a letter to the Gamekeeper Journal in 1889. This was sent by James Miller from Twynholm in Dumfriesshire. He states that he bought one of the retrievers in the south of Ireland and praised the breed for their looks and intelligence. This confirms that at least one of the first retrievers, from Guisachan, and from a litter sired by Nous, or one of his offspring, came to Southern Ireland in the early 1880's. This is some time before the early 1900's of previous reports. From what James Miller wrote these retrievers were also being bred from.

It does appear that John Chisholm and James Miller were possibly connected in some way, or they followed each other around. On the 1871 census James, aged 16, is with John and his wife Ann at an address at Tomich in Glen Affric and listed as a Lodger. This would be before John and Ann move to Aultbeath. On the 1881 census, a John Miller is listed at an address in Affric, age 60 and his occupation is given as Gamekeeper. I have not been able to find where James was at this time, but was John the father of James and did the latter follow his father's occupation? By 1891 James was in Ireland also working on the

Muckross estate as a gamekeeper. His name is mentioned more than once in court cases in the 1890's relating to problems with theft and damage on the estate. Added to this there was general unrest with the eviction of tenants due to the imposition of land tax brought in by the government of the day.

John Chisholm (5th from the left)
By permission of Muckross Archives

During the period that John and James spent at the Muckross estate they no doubt experienced some unsettled times. Despite John being credited with improving the shooting on the estate, Henry Arthur Herbert's financial problems were increasing and in 1890 he rented the shooting to Ralph Sneyd, an English Squire from Staffordshire.

This arrangement lasted for several seasons, but he brought in his own dogs and keepers. It was not long before there was confrontation, with disputes about living accommodation and where the dogs were kennelled in the shooting season. James was also accused, by Ralph Sneyd, of being a poacher and drunkard.

By the end of the decade it appears that James had had enough and returned to Scotland with his wife, Helen, and their three children who had all been born in Ireland. John was also aware that changes were coming. In 1897 Henry Arthur Herbert was bankrupt and all his assets were seized. When the property came up for sale in 1899 it failed to find a buyer. A few weeks later it was bought by Arthur Guinness, the 1st Baron Ardilaun. Throughout this time of change, John remained on the estate but in 1905 he also decided to leave Ireland and returned to Scotland and spent the remainder of his days near Guisachan.

John Chisholm was known as 'The Giant' during the time he was at Muckross and his photo with other estate workers shows that he was well over six foot. He must have been well thought of and remembered by James Miller and others on the estate for the way he trained and worked the 'Tweedmouth' retrievers at Muckross. He brought the first yellow retrievers to Ireland and worked them. In difficult and turbulent times for Ireland they should be congratulated as pioneers of this new breed.

SO, IN THE EARLY YEARS of the breed we know that some of them were worked on the estates around Guisachan. We know that some went to Southern Ireland - with thanks from gamekeepers around Guisachan. So that leaves England - and for those in the early days of the development of the breed this gives something of a conundrum.

John Mawe is a name that does not spring to mind in the history of the breed. The picture of him with a Golden Retriever claims that it was taken in 1880 and that the dog's name was Stella. It also states that Stella was in the ownership of the Earl of Chesterfield. The picture was included in an article published in 1913 and I have some considerable doubts that the date given was correct. There is no question that the dog is a Golden Retriever, but it would not have been called this in 1880. It appears to have been working, with its retrieve in its mouth, and John Mawe, dressed as a gamekeeper, with shooting piece, hunting boots, jacket and headdress for the period - late 1800's, early 1900's. He does look very smart, but was he a gamekeeper?

The photo was taken by a Mr Nunn from Scarborough, but this was nowhere near the family seat of the Chesterfield family at Holme Lacey in Herefordshire. When researching

John Mawe
Our Dogs November 1st 1912

the census for John Mawe it shows that he lived in the same area for all of his seventy years, born, raised, married and died in the area of Kilburn in North Yorkshire. On the census for 1871 it is recorded that he was a gamekeeper but that he was "out of employment". For all the other census years he is recorded as being a dog trainer, with the odd inclusion on the 1881 census of the number "8"! Even his son William at the age of 17 was a dog trainer and he had "8" after his occupation. One assumes that this referred to dogs being trained at the time, but was it "8" each? And, if it had been entered properly, what type of dogs were they? To do the census justice - what were their names?! For all other census years, a number does not appear!

To train dogs for over 40 years he could have been very good at it and well known. At this time, the training would have been for working the dogs, whatever breed, and part of his success could have been to dress as a gamekeeper so that when they were sent back to their owners there would have been an association between trained dog and owner.

If the year given for the photo of 1880 is correct, then it would not have been from the first litter born at Guisachan.

In none of the years that Dudley's stud book was kept does the name of Stella appear. Records from the past do not indicate that the Earl of Chesterfield knew Dudley Coutts Marjoribanks. The Earl's name does not appear on any of the visitor lists for the shooting season at Guisachan, even under the family surname of Scudamore-Stanhope. The family did not have a record of longevity, the 7th, 8th and 9th Earl's - the latter being at the time of John Mawe's photo - dying within sixteen years of each other. It was only the 7th Earl who appears to have had a connection with dogs. He accepted the office of the President of the National Exhibition of Sporting Dogs in 1867, before the first of Dudley' retrievers were born. This Earl was not president for long. He died in 1871.

How Stella came to be with the 9th Earl of Chesterfield and being trained by John Mawe is a mystery, which no doubt will be solved at a future time.

~❧ 3 ❧~

Following the Tail
- or should that be trail?

IN THE SECOND HALF of the 19th century any new breed of dog would have been of interest to those who worked on the land. Gamekeepers would have been foremost in showing interest and if the dogs had been bred with a retrieving instinct then they would soon have come to their attention. The last chapter gave details of the journeymen keepers - and one dog trainer or gamekeeper in particular. There were many more. Aside from the journeyman keepers there were the estates that had their own kennels and in Scotland a lot of these would include retrieving breeds. Some of these would have originated from Guisachan. News of a new breed would have spread quite rapidly. These were the days when people talked to each other and the reputation of the breed would have quickly increased.

Guisachan, its mansion, kennels and stables, is in Glen Affric. Twenty-two miles north in Strathconon is Dalbreac Lodge and Scardale Lodge. These properties also had kennels and stables and had belonged to the Balfour family since about 1845. The kennels were added in 1849 and a new keeper's house was built. From this it is more than likely that some dogs were here all year. For a time, the

Dalbreac Lodge, taken about 1875

shooting grounds were rented to a Mr John La Touche, but when he decided to rent the shooting on another highland estate in 1856, a number of his dogs were sent to auction. These were Setters and Pointers and the auction took place the same year in Dublin.

Despite lengthy research on this property and its surroundings, I have not yet been able to find out if any gamekeepers lived here at this time, or if there were dogs kept here all year, although the building of new kennels makes this a possibility. As the main residence of the Balfour family was Whittingehame House in Berwickshire, it can only be assumed that it was kept as a hunting lodge for the shooting season and that the kennels were only used for part of the year. The owner of both these properties was renowned for being an excellent rifle-shot and stalker. This is somewhat odd as he was also short sighted! Yes, vision!

What is known is that the Balfour family had a round-about connection with dogs, which for a number of generations was centred on the retrievers that had been bred at Guisachan.

The family surname can be traced back to the 17th century and as was normal during the following generations they often repeated forenames or variations of them. In 1815 a James Balfour married Eleanor Maitland. They had a daughter, Mary, who was born in 1817 at Whittinghame. She was to become a renowned artist whose paintings are now much sought after and fetch high prices at auction. She loved country scenes, the grander the better, and when she married in 1837, it was to open a new world for her painting. The person that she married was Henry Arthur Herbert. Remember him? Yes, the same as mentioned in the last chapter - the owner of the Muckross Estate left to him by his father, Henry Arthur Herbert. He must have been fixated by this name, or perhaps it was easy to remember, as the second child of his marriage was a son, and his name was - no surprise - Henry Arthur Herbert!

Henry Arthur Herbert (the 2nd one) must have been delighted that Mary had agreed to marry him as she brought with her a dowry of £40,000, over £3million pounds in today's money. Henry quickly set about spending some of this modernising the estate at Muckross starting with alterations at Torc Cottage overlooking the Lakes of

Killarney. This was to be their family home. Here Mary could paint every day, among other things!

Henry Arthur Herbert (the 2nd) died in 1866, and the estate was left to his first son, Henry Arthur Herbert, the 3rd. He quickly started to spend what money was left and Mary, despite her love of the area around Muckross, decided to move to London in 1871, shortly after the time that John Chisholm took the position of head keeper on the estate and brought with him some of the first yellow retrievers.

Well before this time, Mary's brother, James Maitland Balfour born in 1820, had married, Blanche Mary Gascoyne-Cecil in 1843 and by 1855, they had seven children. Sadly, a year later James died. Mary outlived her brother by almost 40 years. When she went to London she lived for a time with her eldest nephew, Arthur James Balfour. They also stayed at the family home at Whittinghame. In 1869 Arthur James had reached his 'majority' and huge celebrations were held in Strathconon on the 28th and 29th of July. A sports competition took place on the first day with athletic races and prizes for the local children and on the second day a huge dinner for the people living in the area at Dalbreac Lodge. Among them were George Shearlaw, Head Keeper, Dalbreac - proof that by now keepers were resident on this estate. Other keepers had the surname of Collie, Kaye and Macintyre and they all lived on the estate.

By this time the Balfour family had spent a great deal of money in the area on improvements for the people who lived and worked here. All of the properties had been modernised, a new school had been built, and a new road had been laid for the 21 miles from Beauly through Strathconon to link Dalbreac Lodge with Scardroy Lodge, which had been built in 1873, at the far end of Strathconon. At the end of the dinner there was more than one speech that gave praise for what the Balfour family had done for them. All very reminiscent of what the Marjoribanks family had done for the families and workers in Glen Affric some years earlier.

In 1874 Arthur entered parliament as MP for Hertford, and he was soon appointed to several government committees. His visits to the Highlands for the shooting season continued for some years but they were proving to be more difficult as Arthur took on more parliamentary positions. In 1902 he reached the pinnacle of his career when he was appointed prime minister. For rest and relaxation, he chose to spend time at Whittinghame. In the late 1800's Arthur sold the whole of the Strathconon estate to Richard Henry Combe. Did Dudley have a hand in this? Dudley was a director of Meux's brewery in London, as was Harry Meux, and they both had an interest in shooting and dogs. Their friendship was close, and on more than one occasion Harry's dogs appeared on the stud lists.

Richard Henry Combe was a director of Watney Combe Reid, another of the large breweries in London. So, it looks more than likely that when they met up for shooting, they discussed business at their breweries, the outlook for a future shooting season and the progress of their dogs. Their discussions could well have included, *"by the way, do you know of a good shooting estate for sale?"*

Strathconon being bought by Richard Henry Combe would prove to be of huge benefit to the breed. He paid £70,000 for the estate which from the sale documents covered over

60,000 acres. This was mainly shooting and grazing land and included all the properties including Dalbreac Lodge and Scardale Lodge. Forty years prior to this Dudley Coutts Marjoribanks had paid £53,000 for 20,000 acres and seeing that they were similar in terrain and that land prices were reasonably stable it could be that the price paid was very close to each other when inflation is taken into consideration. Either way Richard Henry Combe got what he wanted, and I have no doubt that the estate workers would have been apprehensive with the new owners, but their fears were quickly allayed, and daily life continued as before. The only change that Richard made was to modify and enlarge and to change the name of Dalbreac Lodge to Strathconon House.

Despite the fact that Richard spent a good deal of time at his home in Surrey, which enabled him to look after the business at the brewery in London, he also regularly went to Strathconon. With him on some of these visits was his eldest son Christian Combe, born in 1859, who had chosen a career in the military, achieving the position of Captain in the Lifeguards in 1890. He quickly came to enjoy long days on the hills - very long days in the shooting season. Father and son together, very much like Dudley Coutts Marjoribanks and his son; history repeating itself. And dogs with them? Yes, most certainly. And gamekeepers with them? Yes, most certainly. The details of these days are not as well documented as in the Guisachan days but what we do know, from a brief report in the Our Dogs journal for May 1912, is this: *"Captain Combe, who has a large kennel of the Goldens in Scotland, uses nothing else, and finds them invaluable for tracking wounded deer"*.

Where had the Goldens come from? Any stud lists that had been kept on this estate have not survived, but dogs bred on the estate were given the affix of Strathconon. Without evidence the Combe family did not appear to be interested in registering their dogs, leaving it to others once they had gone to new owners. One of these was a dog by the name of Strathpeffer Stag, sired by Strathconon Laddie in 1913, the dam being Beatidh - the Gaelic for Betty. The new owner of the puppy was a Mr A. Wallace whose address at this time, and for a number of years, was the Strathpeffer Spa Hotel. The breeder was a Mr J. Macdonald.

It is possible that he was a gamekeeper on the Dunrobin Castle estate 40miles north of Strathconon owned by the Duke of Sutherland, but with this surname and in this area, I am unable to prove this - at the moment! After many hours of research, I have found that any Scottish person with a surname that starts with 'Mac' is never easy to trace!! What I do know is that Mr J. Macdonald was not related to Donald Macdonald, the gamekeeper at Ingestre for over 30 years who did so much to make the breed so popular in the days before WW1. One can only assume that Mr J. Macdonald owned (and worked?) Strathconon Laddie; but did he have any other Goldens at this time?

What are the other options as to where these Goldens came from? The most obvious are dogs from the original breeding at Guisachan and for a time carried on by Lord Portsmouth after he bought this estate. Another possibility is that some Goldens came from the Edington estate or that others had been brought back from Southern Ireland with John Chisholm. If the latter had brought them back, were they closely in line related to Nous and his visit to Aultbeath in 1868?

What is certain is that the report of May 1912 is correct and gives proof that the Goldens were being worked on the Strathconon estate by keepers employed by the Combe family and had been well before the date of the report.

Richard Henry Combe died on the 8th of April 1900. The estate was left to his eldest son, Captain Christian Combe. On the 26th July 1883 Christian married Lady Jane Seymour Conyngham and before Richard Henry died he saw all of his four grandchildren from his son's marriage. After Christian finished his military career he spent more time on the Strathconon estate. He had a great interest in shooting and had an ambition to shoot 100 royal stags. Not good news for stags! But he did achieve this in October 1936. By this time he was in his 78th year and up to then he was in excellent health, but he died suddenly on the 11th October 1940. Good news for the stags! Not such good news for the dogs - hopefully still Goldens. His wife survived him but nine months later Strathconon House was totally destroyed by fire and most of the memories that were kept there were lost - perhaps the stud books also. His wife who was in the house at the time survived. I do not know if she suffered any injuries but the loss of her husband and her home in such a short space of time must have affected her and she died on the 30th October 1941 at the age of 81.

Reflecting on what I have been able to find out about the breed and this estate I do feel that there is a lot more to be uncovered. To find that Goldens were used for retrieving and tracking at Strathconon shows how much the breed had developed and been accepted by 1912, and it would be good to prove that they were still being worked here in 1941.

As a coincidence, the surname of Conyngham - an unusual one. This name was Christian Combe's wife's maiden name and it appears in the Charlesworth family line. Mrs C. did say that she got her first Golden from a keeper in Scotland, but then she did also say it was Northumberland - or was it Norfolk?

❧ 4 ❧

Golden is the Fashion

IT CAN NEVER be firmly established as to how quickly the new breed of yellow retriever was recognised as a reliable and easily trained dog. For obvious reasons it was at first kept at a low level - dogs take time to breed and raise their offspring - and there is no doubt that Dudley Coutts Marjoribanks did restrict where the few dogs at this time went. Although he recognised that he had brought to the dog world a breed that had great potential for its working ability he was also more than willing to give his support to events that promoted all breeds. One of these was the annual Inverness Show of Dogs usually held in the month of September. In 1874 it was held in a large railway shed at Lochgorm next to the Highland Railway line from Inverness to Dingwall. Dudley was one of the main promoters of the show. Was it coincidence that he was also a director of the Highland Railway company at this time?

The show attracted over 220 entries - and that was the total number of dogs! Amongst them were dogs classified as retrievers - 16 curly and 8 wavy. I doubt if any of these were from the original litters of yellow retrievers bred at Guisachan but that cannot be proved. At this time any dog show generated great interest. Some entrants were prepared to travel miles in the hope of their dog winning a moment of glory and outshining all the others even if they were not Golden!

In the late 1800's classes were often judged as breed groups and it would only be after 1885 that classes would become more specific with regard to colour and if they were dogs or bitches. These changes were to continue and remain into the 1900's. Shows were also to become specific in classes for those who were exhibiting. It also became a way of bringing breeds that had not been seen before to the attention of the dog loving fraternity. This would very much benefit the Goldens and it was the gamekeepers who took full advantage of this. At several of the biggest shows, including Crufts, there were classes only for gamekeepers' dogs and time was set aside for the sale of dogs. Despite the fact that Crufts was held in London, it did not get in the

Possibly taken c1882 of Majorie Adeline Gordon, 1st Daughter of John Campbell Hamilton-Gordon, and Ishbel, nee Marjoribanks. The dark colour of the breed was often referred to as 'red'

way of taking dogs to be sold or for taking orders for puppies from the next planned litters.

Away from the shows there was still a great deal of interest in working them and at these events the Goldens were gaining steady recognition. Showing and working them bridged the gap between the gentry and the working class. There were many of them in this group and the breed attracted dog lovers from various backgrounds, and the few mentioned here all played their part in making the new breed an attractive addition to the dog world. It is fitting that one of the first of these chose Scotland as his home for training and showing.

A̲RTHUR G̲ERVAISE H̲ENDLEY was born in India on the 26th June 1866. His father, John, was a surgeon in the Indian Army Medical Service and Arthur in time would follow him into the medical field. His education and initial training in medicine took place in Britain and by 1887 he had qualified as a Member of the Royal College of Surgeons - MRCS - at St. Bart's Hospital in London. Father and son now qualified in the medical world with Arthur following his father into the Indian Army as a medical

LT.-Col. Hendley with a group of Golden Retrievers at Pitfar, Dollar, N.B.

officer. For the next 20 years he was based in India, although he did return to Britain regularly. On one of these visits he had an important appointment to attend to. This was in 1898 when he got married to Jessie Grahame Petrie in Eastbourne. This grand event was followed by a honeymoon in Western Ireland. Did they see retrievers here - offspring of the Tweedmouth retrievers brought over by John Chisholm years earlier? When they returned to India they started a family, and, when they were old enough, the children were sent to Britain to be educated.

Arthur ended the first part of his Army career - there was more to come - in 1909 by which time he had attained the rank of Lieutenant Colonel. On returning to Britain he took the position on a part time basis of Medical lecturer at Trinity College, Glen Almond, Perthshire. He lived at a property called Pitfar, near Dollar, Perthshire. This had extensive grounds which were large enough for him to return to his love of dogs which had started while he was in India. Fox Terriers and Airedales he had found to be best suited to the Indian climate. No Goldens here, but they were soon to be at Pitfar. They arrived once the Colonel had built new kennels and the first of them were from the redoubtable Mrs Charlesworth. Where they first met is not known but it was more than likely that it was at a dog show and more than likely that Mrs Charlesworth was impressed by his clear sightedness with regards to dogs and his organised thoughts on the breeds at the show. These were attributes which had been mentioned during his medical work. Mrs Charlesworth took note of this.

No surprise that Arthur was one of the first presidents of the Golden Retriever Club formed in 1913. Mrs C did her marketing very well! She sold him his first dogs and got him on the first committee! These people are still in the dog world today! But the training of the dogs was down to the Colonel and before long he found them so easy to train that by 1911 all the Labradors that he started with had been dispersed; evicted - got rid of! The Goldens had moved in!

Lieutenant Colonel Hendley was soon promoting the breed, firstly in Scotland and then south of the border. His affix of Pitfar was entered on the registrations of many of the litters from 1913 to 1916. His name appeared being placed with his dogs at field trials; the Kennel Club trials 1913 and the Scottish trials at Lochinch in the same year -

and shows - Crufts in 1914 and 1916 and the Ladies Kennel Association Show held at the Ranelagh Club Gardens in London, also in 1916. In a short time he was regarded as an authority of the breed, especially north of the border.

All his good work with promoting the breed came to a sudden end. The First World War at this time appeared to be never ending and with the increasing shortage of fighting men, and men to treat the wounded, the Colonel answered the call to return to his medical duties of the past. For the next two years he was based at Woolwich and could well have been alongside Mrs Charlesworth who by this time was also giving part of her time to the war effort. When the war finally came to an end the Colonel returned to Pitfar. During the time that he was away it is not known if his Goldens were being looked after by someone else at Pitfar but he did register a dog in 1919 bred by the ever reliable Donald Macdonald, the Gamekeeper at Ingestre. There is no record that he added any more dogs after this and for some reason he ended his involvement with the dog world.

Lieutenant Colonel Hendley died on the 18th of September 1932 at the age of 66. His address was given as Birkhill, Muckhart, Dollar, which is assumed to be Pitfar. However, I have checked this from more than one source, and on the 1st of September 1932 the contents of this property were sold and when he died he only left £623 10s 7d to his widow Jessie. The relatively small amount indicates that Pitfar did not belong to the Colonel but was rented from Trinity College. When Jessie died is not known.

For the short time that Lieutenant Colonel Hendley was in the dog world he did play an important role in supporting the development of the breed.

THE SAME CAN ALSO BE SAID for Rhona Crawshay whose life appears to have been one of relative leisure, living on her own and on her own means, no employment but more than likely in poor health for part of her short life.

Her family were part of what was known by the mid-19th century as the Welsh Iron Masters, which comprised many manufacturing companies in South Wales at this time. They were all family run and the owners became very wealthy. When Rhona's Grandfather, Robert Thompson Crawshay died in 1879 he left £1.6 million pounds. This is over £61 million pounds today!

This money was divided between Robert's three sons, the youngest of which was Richard Frederick Crawshay. In 1880 he married Tempe (or Tempi?) Isabella Oakes and by 1888 they had one son and three daughters, the youngest of which was Rhona who was born on the 12th June of that year. By this time the family had moved to London although they still owned Ty Mawr near Abergavenny which they used mainly in the summer months, but they were at this address on the 1901 census. Within the next decade there were considerable changes in family life for

Rhona. On the 25th of October 1903 her father died in Bournemouth, at the age of 44, from a lung condition that he had been suffering from for many years.

Then on the 19th of May 1906 her elder sister, Leila, died in France at the age of 21. Added to this by 1911 Rhona had moved out of London to a property named Newlands, Nr Hitchin, Hertfordshire. She was living on her own and by her own means and she had six servants to do everything for her. Her mother, still in London, had dogs, Black Pugs, which she bred, and for a time she was on the committee of the Ladies Kennel Association. Rhona decided to follow her mother and had a dog - even better it was a Golden Retriever. On the 11th of July she registered a dog by the name of Rusty Rover bred by a Mr Usher. Later that year she registered a bitch by the name of Gosmore Birdie. She adopted Gosmore as her affix for future litters, the name being from a nearby village where she lived. Gosmore Birdie was from a litter bred by - you guessed it - Mrs Charlesworth's Normanby Beauty, using Lord Harcourt's Culham Brass as the sire.

Like many others, Rhona was delighted with what was still

Rhona's first litter of puppies born in 1913 at Newlands, one of which is no doubt Gosmore Vesta. The name of the kennel man is not known.

a relatively new breed and she added to them by breeding three litters with her own dogs, keeping those that she was possibly advised were the best and selling others. She also attended numerous shows and field trials and was placed with the dogs that she showed and worked on many occasions. She first showed at Crufts in 1912 with Rusty Rover but the dog was not placed. But she was determined to show one of the dogs that she had bred, and win at a Championship show. And this she did at Crufts in 1915 with Gosmore Vesta - a two-year-old dog. By this year her puppies were much sought after, and they were noted for their even appearance and alertness from an early age. In the same year they drew the attention of a Mr Winter-Jenkin from Melbourne, Australia who attended Crufts and purchased Gosmore Nugget, a dog, and took in back to the other side of the world. The reports of this dog were extremely favourable to such an extent that he purchased another puppy, which survived the long sea journey and after its arrival gave equal satisfaction for many years.

In November 1915 she announced that she was giving up on the breed and the dog world. She cited the reason for doing this that now she had achieved her ambition to win a championship with a dog of her own breeding that it was time for her to leave. All her dogs were put up for sale. Despite winning at numerous shows and field trials this did not happen quickly and it took over nine months for them to go to new homes. She attended her last show in January 1916 at the National Gundog Society Show held in London where Gosmore Kestral was placed second in the Golden class for open dogs. I do have some doubts as to the reason why she left the dog world at this time. Some months before she gave up the breed, she had been elected onto the newly formed Golden Retriever Club Committee so by withdrawing from the dog world there was already a vacancy. Another possible reason may have been that she turned her attention to the war effort as in 1917 she was doing work for the Red Cross collecting clothes for soldiers returning from the front. It may also have been because of health problems. For many years she had a nurse with her, either where she lived or on her journeys to shows and field trials.

Although she left the dog world, she did not leave dogs completely. In December 1919, she was charged by the police in Amersham, Buckinghamshire with three offences - for allowing a dog to stray onto the road, not having a dog under control and for not having a muzzle on the dog. I have not been able to find what the breed of the dog was! For this she had to attend the petty sessions where she was fined five shillings for each of the offences. At this time she gave her address as Coleshill, but by 1925 she was on the electoral register living at Hertfordshire House although this could have been the new name for Newlands.

Two years later, and possibly recovered from any health problems, she had another Golden, registered by the name of Donkelve Jester which had been born in 1926. Its great grandfather was Normanby Balfour - thanks to Mrs Charlesworth; had she kept in touch with her? Sadly, this dog was not to be with Rhona for very long, although I hope it gave her great pleasure while she had it, as in 1931 Rhona died at the age of 43 at the Falmouth Hotel in Cornwall. The cause of death was a ruptured coronary artery. She also had lung cancer.

In her will, published in 1932 she left £9,901.00 and in keeping with other wills made by the Crawshay family in the past she gave several small amounts to people who had looked after her during her lifetime. The one beneficiary that is puzzling, was to a Janet McDowall at Crossburn in Dumfriesshire, Scotland. Had Rhona stayed here and seen her first Goldens here? Were they from James Miller who returned from Southern Ireland to Dumfriesshire? Were they offspring of the Guisachan puppies? Still more to find out.

A week before I completed this section on Rhona for the book, I had a phone call from a woman in Herefordshire who directed me to a website and a journal about canals and longboats published in 2015. In it was a picture of a silver hallmarked dog whistle with the name, R. Crawshay engraved on it. It was found in a workshop at a property near Lydney, in a box of rubbish. How it found its way here is a mystery. As I said - still more to find out.

Rhona was certainly not rubbish. In her short time she also contributed hugely to the development and promotion of the breed and she deserves full credit for it.

DESPITE THE FACT that Rhona decided to leave the dog world after a relatively short time there were now others to fill her place and continue to promote the breed. One of these was Lucy Ada Jervis, better known in the show ring and at field trials as Lady Harris. She was born in Cheshire in 1851. Her parents were Carnegie Robert John Jervis, the 3rd Viscount Saint Vincent of Meaford and Lucy Charlotte Baskervye-Glegg. By 1860 they had seven children all born in Cheshire. A year later they had moved to Godmersham Park near Faversham in Kent, where over time they added another three children to the family.

No doubt they were wealthy, so much so that they employed a governess to look after the children's education. Details of Lucy's life after what would be classed as her informative years are somewhat sketchy but it is known that she was a great lover of the countryside around Godmersham and it was in this area that she met the other great love of her life - her future husband. He was George Robert Canning Harris, the 4th Baron Harris of Seringapatam and Mysore. They were married on the 8th July 1874. Her new home was Belmont House near Throwley in Kent, ten miles from Godmersham.

She was to live here for the remainder of her life and having visited this property I can understand why. The grounds cover over 3,000 acres and it is without doubt as peaceful now as it was in her days. During the first years of her marriage the time that she was able to spend at Belmont was limited as she made several long visits to India to support her husband who had been appointed Governor of Bombay. She played her part in the social life of the area and her husband's love of cricket soon made them a popular couple. They did make several brief visits back to their home at Belmont and it was here that their only son, George St. Vincent was born on the 3rd September 1889. His early years were spent with his parents in India. Before leaving India for the last time and for service to the community Lady Harris was awarded with the order of the Crown of India. They returned to Belmont in 1895 where they could fully enjoy their home and the countryside.

From her childhood days Lady Harris had loved dogs, all dogs and all breeds. It was not until 1910 that we have proof of one of the breeds that she kept. This the Airedale Terrier and one of these by the name of Gypsy she showed at Crufts in 1910. She returned in 1912 showing Spaniels and a year later she showed her Spaniels and her Pekingese. 1912 was probably the year that was to be of benefit to the development of the Golden Retriever. At the Ladies Kennel Association show, held at Regents Park for this year, she showed a year-old bitch by the name of Normanby Belinda, with which she gained a reserve in the Junior Class. No prizes for knowing where she got this dog from. Mrs Charlesworth promoting the breed again and I have no doubt that Lady Harris and Mrs C. would have got on well as it has often been said that the latter enjoyed mingling with titled people.

The following year Lady Harris showed at this venue again this time with her dog Goldie, which was out of the first litter of Goldens that she bred. She must have been pleased with Goldie showing her at Crufts in 1914 and although she was not placed, she returned to Crufts the following year but not to show her dogs. It appears to have been to advertise the breed and to sell other Goldens that she bred from 1915 to 1919. Bred with the affix Belmont, these puppies must have attracted buyers, as several dogs that were entered in succeeding years carried this affix in their breed line. In this way she did promote the breed but with changes to the country brought about by WW1 it was becoming increasingly difficult to look after any breed of dog. But in this Lady Harris had an alternative. She was able to turn her interest from showing to working and she arranged for field trials at Belmont and at her first home in Kent, Godmersham Park. The trial that she arranged in 1921, was just for Goldens, and reported as being the best ever arranged - and yes, Mrs Charlesworth attended.

Working her dogs and making it possible for other lovers of the breed to work theirs would have given Lady Harris great satisfaction and after the war she had no desire to return to showing or to Crufts. She did immerse herself in giving support to organisations in and around Belmont and was well known in the village of Throwley and the towns of Faversham and Sittingbourne. Throughout what can be claimed as her retirement at Belmont she also supported her husband with his commitment to Kent County Cricket Club and by reports on him he was very good at this sport.

Lady Harris died on 19th February 1930 at the age of 78. Up until this time she had enjoyed good health but after what was thought to be a minor operation, she died of

THE GOLDEN RETRIEVER FIELD TRIAL AT GODMERSHAM PARK

A party assembled at Godmersham Park, the joint residence of Viscount Lewisham and Major L.Palmer, prior to the Retriever Trials. Shows Lord Lewisham with three of his children. November 1921

heart failure in a nursing home at Faversham. There were still Goldens at Belmont when she passed away and they were well looked after by later generations of the Harris family, and some of the Goldens who had passed away before her were also remembered, being buried in the grounds of Belmont. Among them is Goldie, her first Golden Retriever, such is the love she had for the breed. Her headstone is still there today to commemorate her.

By coincidence in that same year Frederick Carnegie Lowe died on the 8th September 1930. He and his three wives (not all at once!) had been lifelong friends with the Harris family. Best known in the dog world as F.C. Lowe he was well respected as a judge and a trainer of working dogs, the Spaniel being his preferred breed. He was very popular with dogs of all breeds, even the mongrel, as he owned a factory near Sittingbourne, which made food for animals. One of the brand names that he used was 'Carta Carna'. These two words are taken from the Hindustani language and translates to 'Dog's Food'. With the Harris's connection with India, one wonders who thought of this name?

TIME MOVES ON. Those who I have written about - and there were others - were aware that the world was changing and that rumours of conflict between countries was growing. The first to feel the effects of this were the gamekeepers who had done so much to make the breed acceptable to the dog world as a working asset. These men were the first to heed the call to arms and were welcomed by the services as they were well trained with a rifle. Sadly, many of them would die on the field of battle and would no longer return to enjoy a day's shooting with this wonderful breed. And those that I have written about were also willing to reluctantly give up the breed for a time to add their experience already gained to assist the war effort. Someone who did her best to support the breed for as long as she could and who does not appear to have gained much credit for doing so was Beatrice Mary Maud Hall.

Beatrice Mary Maud Hall was born in September 1872 at Aldershot, Hampshire. Her father was Colonel Montagu Hall, who married Emily Simmonds in 1869. By 1891 they had had eight children, Beatrice being the second eldest. For most of this time, her father was with the 1st Royal Munster Fusiliers and the children were born at or near army encampments around the country. The family must have been used to frequent moves and Beatrice and her brothers and sisters first appeared on the census in 1891, when Beatrice was 19. None of them are listed with an occupation and the three youngest children are not listed as being scholars. It was the same ten years later - no occupation. Perhaps they were all enjoying the seaside as by this time their father had retired, and they were living on the Isle of Wight.

On the 12th of March 1904 Beatrice's father died at the family home at the age of 72. His funeral and burial took place at Winchester Cathedral a few days later. Among those who attended were many from his regiment, and servicemen who knew him. Also, family members, but Beatrice was not one of them. The reason is not known. The next time that there was news of her was when she got married - happier times. She was married on the 28th February 1911. The groom was Robert Henry Ames. He was a Lieutenant in the Royal Navy and was stationed on H.M.S Hannibal Devonport.

Wherever Beatrice was before the marriage is not known

but she may have come to London days before the wedding as her address on the certificate was the Granville Hotel in Marylebone, London. The wedding took place at St. James Catholic church by licence. This could explain why Beatrice came from a family of eight and still kept to this faith. After the wedding, Robert Henry returned to Devonport within days, hours even. The wedding was witnessed by Beatrice's mother, Emily and by Robert's mother Margaret, with whom Beatrice lived for a time in South Kensington, London, after the wedding. One other witness to the marriage is also on the certificate. That was Robert's father, Louis Eric Ames. Added to his name on the certificate is 'Belhaven and Stenton'. This refers to the area where he lived for many years and straddles Northumberland and Berwickshire, both areas with strong Golden Retriever connections. But it was not this breed that Beatrice is recorded as showing at first.

In 1914 she showed her Irish Setters at the Richmond Show and in the same year she exhibited these same dogs at the Plymouth show. It could have been in the same year that she acquired her first Golden Retriever by the name of Rust Boy. This dog had been bred by Mr W.S. Hunt, and it was born on the 1st June 1914, the dog for this litter being Normanby Balfour. Mrs Charlesworth having her effect on the breed again! Two years later Beatrice showed this dog at Crufts where it was awarded third place in the limit class. It was the address that she gave for exhibitors that was somewhat intriguing which was "The Hut, K Lines, Curragh Camp, Co. Kildare".

A year later she was back at Crufts and she gave another address. This time it was Glanduff Castle, Broadford, Charleville, Co. Limerick. The report of this, found in the issue of the Shooting Times dated July 21st, 1917, adds the information that she and her husband were now

Glanduff Tinker

permanently at this address. This could have been reported for the benefit of the people that they knew in the dog world as they often moved around. I do not believe that this was the first time that they lived here, but it would appear it was here that the kennels were, with the numbers of dogs kept having been reduced somewhat due to the war. And the Crufts show for 1917 also gave something of a surprise - no Setters shown. In their place Beatrice showed two Fox Terriers, but fear not, she also showed Goldens!

Like many others she had to give up showing at other events until 1921 when Crufts returned, and at this show she exhibited Goldens and Setters but no Fox Terriers. Another address appeared in the show catalogue, this time The Sundridge Mansion House, Bromley, Kent. After a two-year break, she showed again in 1924 giving her address as The Elms, Harlington, Middlesex. This time she showed Setters but, named with her in the show catalogue, was a Dr. P. Coffey. What was he doing with her? Before anyone makes any assumptions the only Dr. P. Coffey that I have found that would fit the bill at this time and lived in Co. Limerick was a Roman Catholic Priest - is that anything to go by? Just to confuse matters further the entry below The Elms gives a Mrs R. Ames with the address of c/o Grindley & Co. 54 Parliament Street S.W.1. She showed a Golden named Sergeant of Kentford, bred by the Hon. Mrs Grigg out of Normanby Campfire and two Setters with the affix Glanduff. Surely the same person - with or without Dr. P. Coffey.

1924 was the last year that Mrs Ames showed her dogs at Crufts. Sadly, she died on the 8th of July 1927 at the age of 55, at the Anglo-American Clinic in Nice, France near where she lived at the time. The cause of her death is not known. She left the small amount that she had to her husband, Lieutenant-commander, Robert Henry Ames, who had retired from the Royal Navy. He died in 1930, aged 46, following injuries sustained in a road accident.

Mrs Ames has been the most difficult person to research for this book. So why include her? Because for her sheer determination to keep her dogs throughout the war and to show them during difficult times. And when she returned to show at Crufts, she would have seen many new faces and new dogs to take the breed forward for the future.

THOSE WHO PROMOTED the new breed from 1900 to 1920 quickly gained a deep admiration for them and were quick to recognise their qualities. There were a few others that I have not included but all of the above worked and showed their dogs and were prepared to travel many miles to exhibit them. When Col. Hendley, Rhona Crawshay, Lady Harris and Mrs Ames, were joined by Donald Macdonald, Lord Harcourt and Mrs Charlesworth at shows and working events, they must have had plenty to

Goldens making a fine picture at the Ladies Kennel Association show, Regents Park London 1913. Among the handlers, 2nd from left, Miss Rhona Crawshay, 5th from left, Lady Harris, next to her, Mrs Charlesworth and at the far end the judge Major-General Vesey Dawson.

talk about with regards to the merits of this wonderful breed. After the shows they no doubt shared a glass or two of beer or a glass or two of Pimms. Which of them enjoyed which drink is anyone's guess!

~৯ 5 ৯~

The Other Theory
- or Tall Stories?

IN THE 1880's a registration system for breeders of all pedigree dogs, was established by the Kennel Club to record the name of the puppies born in a litter. Also included was the date that they were born and who the Dam and Sire of the puppies were. These rules were not mandatory at this time but many breeders who were proud of their breed and the puppies that were bred, were in favour of this ruling. The breeders were also responsible for choosing an affix to the name of the puppies and this was usually the name or the area where the breeder lived. Others chose something not connected, as was the case with the affix of St. Hubert. This Christian saint lived from 658 AD to 727 AD and he was the patron saint of dogs, useful information for all dogs at any time! St. Hubert was the affix that was used by Colonel the Hon. William Le

Colonel the Honourable W. Le Poer Trench, C.V.O.,
Member of the Committee of the Kennel Club

Poer Trench who throughout his life was adamant that the Golden Retriever that we know today originated from Russia.

William Le Poer Trench was born on the 17th June 1837 at Ballinasloe, County Galway. He was the third son of William Thomas Le Poer Trench, the 3rd Earl of Clancarty, and his wife, formally Lady Sarah Juliana Butler. His early years of education were with tutors at Garbally House, the home of his parents, overlooking Ballinasloe. Prior to his teenage years he went to Cheltenham College to complete his education and then to the Royal Military Academy at Woolwich. The latter set him on the way to a short but distinguished career in the Army. He joined the Royal Engineers in 1854 and for the next fifteen years he was employed mainly on Ordnance Survey, which took him to France and Belgium and also to China with the Expeditionary Force, prior to what was to become the Opium War. Here he was involved in active service commanding a ladder regiment between 1857 and 1859. By the time that he left the military he had obtained the rank of Colonel.

In 1864 he married Harriet Maria Georgina Martins and they bought a house near Hyde Park which was to be their London home for over thirty years. Their first son, William was born in 1866 and the second son, Power Mash, was born in 1869. The origins of the forenames of the second son, comes from the old Irish lineage of the Le Poer family going back over three centuries. On leaving the military in 1871 the Colonel stood for Parliament in the same year and was elected the member for Galway. His election was not without controversy and a challenge was made by a Captain Nolan, who also contested the seat. The situation centred on bribes and incorrect election practices but when the case was heard before Judge Keogh he found in favour of the Colonel.

Being born and brought up in Ireland and with his military career it was not long before the Colonel was chosen by the Chief Secretary for Ireland, Sir Michael Hicks Beach, to appoint him as his private secretary, but by 1874, he resigned from parliament after he received an offer to be chairman of the Poor Law and Lunacy Commission in Ireland. By the mid 1880's he had left this commission and chose to spend more time with his other great love in life -

his dogs. Like all things that he was interested in, he wholeheartedly committed himself to the world of dogs. This was to be to the benefit of dogs in general, but also gives some problems to anyone researching what he was claiming about a certain breed.

His first move in following a new lifestyle was to purchase a house outside of London. In 1886 he bought Langley Lodge, near Gerrards Cross in Buckinghamshire, which had 12 rooms and 20 acres of land, well suited for his dogs and for entertaining guests. He still kept his London property, so it was convenient for him to get out to the country at weekends. One of the first tasks at his new country seat was to re-name it St Hubert's. To assist in taking care of his dogs and their early training he employed a gamekeeper by the name of Frederick Almond, who lived on the estate with his wife and children. It is possible that he already resided here prior to the Colonel taking up residence. The whole of the Almond family worked on the estate and all of them must have been trusted and valued, as years later they were left money when the Colonel died.

The first dogs that he had were Irish Water Spaniels, and it would be safe to assume that he would have known a good deal about these through his childhood in Southern Ireland. His knowledge of the breed was to assist him in winning in several shows he entered. The most prominent of these was the Warwickshire Show in 1887 where he took first prize in the class for the Irish Water Spaniel with his dog, Harp. He also had a number of Field Spaniels which he showed but he was not successful with these in the ring.

His Spaniels were not the only dogs that he had in the 1880's. He claimed that in 1883 Lord Ilchester had

Russian Retrievers bred by Col. Le Poer Trench at St Hubert's With Frederick Almond

presented him with a 'Yellow Russian Retriever' by the name of Sandy. This dog was showing signs of 'deterioration' and that the breed was in need of new blood. It was not long before the Colonel took action. He wrote to his contacts in Russia to obtain new stock! How many visits he made to Russia - often abortive - is not known, but from reports it was quite a lot, and over a number of years. One can only admire the Colonel at this time as the areas where he went often near the Caucasian mountains, were at the time not the safest. If you don't succeed at first - try, try again. And the Colonel did - but in what year?

He claimed that the retriever dog he obtained and called Rock, was purebred. A year later he obtained a bitch, which he called May, again claimed to be purebred and which was an Albino. Again - in what year? These dogs were mated but none of the puppies from the litter carried any signs of Albino markings. By 1910, he had a number of 'pure bred' Russian Retrievers which he had bred and registered with the Kennel Club using the affix St. Hubert's and with the grand title - Marjoribanks and Ilchester breed of Yellow Retrievers of Russian origin (imported from Russia in Asia

1858). The Colonel arranged for a standard of points to be drawn up for this breed by Major Harding Cox, a trusted expert on all dogs at this time. This was approved in 1912 by Lord Tweedmouth, the Earl of Ilchester and himself, and by the Kennel Club, and they were included in classes at Crufts in February of that year.

The Colonel entered five dogs in four different classes. In the open class, out of St. Hubert's Rock and St. Hubert's May, born on the 16th January 1911, there was St. Hubert's Peter, Prince, Fritz, Paul and Vesta; St. Hubert's Peter being placed first. As these outnumbered the other dogs in the class it is not surprising that they were placed.

In June of 1912 the Colonel also showed four dogs at the Ladies Kennel Association show held at Regents Park. The dogs shown at this venue were St. Hubert's Prince, Peter, Vesta and Paul. All of these dogs were placed, with Paul taking first prize. There was one other entry in this class listed with a Mrs Calley. It was a dog by the name of Bumble, born in April 1903. It was bred by "the late Lord Ilchester - pedigree unknown". On the day both were 'absent'. I very much hope that dog and handler had not met with a mishap!

The following year, St Hubert's Peter, Paul, Jester, and Prince were again shown at Crufts. There were other retrievers with other handlers in the classes, but it appears that there was some confusion amongst the entrants with regard which class they should have gone into. This situation was rectified the next year, 1914, with a slight alteration to the class description, which was headed, Yellow Russian Retriever. One person who appears to have been confused, in 1913, was Mr G. Marjoribanks. He showed a dog by the name of Lofty which was bred by Captain Loftus who at this time was well known for breeding retrievers. For the record, George Marjoribanks lived in London, worked at Coutts Bank and was a cousin to Edward Marjoribanks. George was born at the Lees in Coldstream, Berwickshire. With all of this one would have thought he knew which class to enter!

The same year the Colonel was back showing at the LKA show in June. This time he showed Prince, Paul, and Vesta all from the litter out of Rock and May. There was one other dog, St Hubert's Czar, born out of Rock and Vesta on the 7th May 1909. With the exception of Czar the others were all placed. And Mrs Calley! No mishap! She made it with Bumble, all the way from Swindon. Sadly, Mrs Calley's dog was not placed but I very much hope that Bumble enjoyed his day out!

The Colonel showed his dogs again at Crufts in 1914. Only one other handler showed a dog for the class of Yellow Russian Retrievers. This was Mr W. G. Waldron who showed Farnborough Duke. The catalogue states that the dog was born on the 16th January 1911, out of the same litter of which the Colonel showed. Mr Waldron gave no address but seeing that Farnborough was not far away, he could have lived near St. Hubert's.

In 1915 there were five classes at Crufts for Russian Retrievers and all the dogs entered belonged to the Colonel. The usual dogs that he had were there, but three others are notable. These were St. Hubert's Ida, Sheela and Koska. They were born on 15th December 1913 from a litter out of St. Hubert's Vesta and Rhona Crawshay's dog Gosmore Freeman. The latter dog had won many prizes at shows and field trials and was no doubt admired by the Colonel.

The following year, no Russian Retrievers were shown, although the Colonel's name was listed as one of the committees Vice Presidents. His name was listed again in the show catalogue for 1917 but again he showed none of his Russian Retrievers. Due to the problems that the country was facing as the First World War dragged on, and the criticism that Charles Cruft was getting for holding the show at this time, he bowed to pressure, so there were no shows from 1918 to 1920. The Colonel had shown his dogs for the last time and by 1920 had attended his last dog show.

IT WILL NEVER be known why the Colonel decided not to show his dogs after 1915 but in the last years of his life he experienced a good deal of sadness. The outbreak of war could well have brought back to him unhappy memories of his time in the military. Other factors could have also played a part. His youngest son William Martins had died in September 1904 at the early age of 38. He had been working as an advisor to the Earl of Carrington which for a time took him to Australia and Canada. He travelled back to this country in the August of 1904, but on landing at Liverpool he was rushed to the main hospital and was diagnosed with malarial blood poisoning. He died within two days of landing.

On the 26th February 1909, the Colonel's wife died suddenly at their London home. She had been treated for some time by several doctors for tuberculosis. She was buried, alongside her son in the family vault in the village of Fulmer, three miles from St.Hubert's. Losing his wife appears to have affected his health. His doctors advised that it would be beneficial to him if he went abroad for a time, and this he did, spending a month in South Africa in early 1911. This was not entirely successful and after he returned to England he had to spend nearly two months at St. Hubert's due to an unknown illness. This was not to be the last time that he was forced to be, as he called it, "imprisoned at St. Hubert's", as in April of 1913 he fell down the stairs at Baker Street underground station. I do feel he was rather harsh in saying he was "imprisoned" at St. Hubert's - surely his dogs were pleased he was at home?

From this set back he did make a full recovery and was back to full fitness after six weeks. It was good to know that he did appear to have regained his health and was able, once again, to play an active part in the dog world - for a time.

We know that he showed his dogs for the last time at Crufts in 1915 but he was still named as being on the committee of the Kennel Club until 1917. He resigned his position in 1918. His last years were spent at St. Hubert's, with his memories, and the dogs, who had been great company for him for many years.

He died on September 16th, 1920, aged 83. Present at his death was his eldest son, Power Mash Le Poer Trench. His death certificate states that he died of Senile Decay. These days it would be classed as Dementia. His burial took place on the 20th September and he was laid to rest beside his wife in the burial plot in Fulmer churchyard. A considerable number of mourners attended the funeral, but it did not include any recognisable name from the dog world.

His will was published on the 7th April 1921. His estate was valued at £92,560 15s 2d. The bulk of this, including the property of St. Hubert's, went to his surviving son. There were several amounts given to those who had worked on his estate for a number of years with his gamekeeper, Mr Almond, being left £800.00. His daughters, who worked at the dairy on the farm, were also left small amounts. In total sixteen former employees were remembered.

The most harrowing request appears on the second page of the will. This states *"I give to my said son my dear yellow retrievers in full confidence that if he cannot arrange to use or breed them himself or place them with good kind masters he will have them chloroformed and buried under my lawn"*.

Sadly, it appears none of his dogs survived.

How many dogs the Colonel had when he died cannot be

confirmed but the litter that was out of Rock and May were born on the 15th January 1911 so any surviving from this litter would have been nine years old and possibly still alive.

Why did his will state "dear yellow retrievers"? No mention of "Russian"?

FROM MY RESEARCH with regard to the Colonel, it is my opinion that he was somewhat economical with the truth. A number of reports in the journals of the time often conflict with what we now know. During his life he contributed to the dog world in many ways. He was involved with Irish Water Spaniels and Field Spaniels, being elected to the committee of both breeds and drawing up the standard for the Irish Water Spaniel. When he turned his attention to the Yellow Retriever he was adamant that the dogs came from Russia and that this is where the Golden Retrievers came from. For over thirty years this claim was mentioned many times.

As time went by, more details came to light, often conflicting as to what had already been known or reported. This did not stop the Colonel from making visits to Russia attempting to find new 'stock'. Despite the fact that he did eventually succeed in his quest, the breed never made the progress that he hoped it would. The gamekeepers did not take to the breed, citing the reason that although they were fine looking dogs that they were quite cumbersome, and their thick coats prevented them from getting into any

The Russian Yellow Retriever, St. Hubert's Peter, winner of Championship at Cruft's Show. Bred by the Hon. Colonel le Poer Trench.

dense undergrowth to retrieve game. They also lacked stamina compared to the Golden Retrievers which would work all day.

I have never found a report that he entered a field trial with his dogs, although I have reason to believe that he did go to Scotland for the shooting season on at least one occasion. In the show ring it was often the case that it was only him with his dogs being judged. Few of the puppies he bred were sold to others in the dog world. He was successful in giving at least one dog away. In April 1913, St. Hubert's Peter was given to His Majesty King George V. I have not found a report as to what His Majesty thought of the dog!

When, with the assistance of Mr Harding Cox, he drew up the standard of points for what would be known as the Russian Yellow Retriever, he sought the approval of the points from two others. The first of these was Lord Marjoribanks. He did not say it was the 3rd Lord - Dudley Churchill Marjoribanks. He was the son of Edward Marjoribanks who had walked with his father on the Sussex Downs in 1864, meeting Obidiah Miles on the way. As far as I am aware Dudley Churchill never had the enthusiasm for the dogs that his father or grandfather had. His interest was in playing Polo or enjoying a day's coursing.

The other person who was given a copy was the 5th Earl of Ilchester who had been given Ada in 1868. The 5th Earl was related by marriage to the Marjoribanks family. Part of the above details have already been given in this book but why would the Colonel give these copies of the proposed new breed of dog when they were quite familiar with dogs of a very similar breed already approved by the Kennel Club. He often repeated the story that the Golden Retriever originated from a 'troupe' of dogs bought at a circus in Brighton. This theory is related time and again but few of them quote the same date. The Colonel must have convinced many in the dog world (even Mrs Charlesworth) about the origins of the first dogs - although Mrs C gave conflicting reports as to where she obtained her first Golden.

As with many claims in history the truth will often come to be known eventually. In July 1952 an article written by the 6th Earl of Ilchester, was published in the Country Life journal. This is a lengthy article and clearly relates the origins of the breed. It also includes the picture with the Earl's father shown on page 9 with Ada. He confirms that the original dog was bought from a shoemaker and that he had obtained this dog from a gamekeeper at Brighton. The Earl also confirms that it was mated to a Tweed Water Spaniel. He acknowledges that other stories of how the breed came to the canine world have been given but they are not backed up by the facts.

The Country Life article refers to the frequent visits made by Col. William Le Poer Trench to Russia, in an attempt by him to prove that they originated from the troupe of dogs at Brighton. He goes on to give further details of the various myths that surround the origins of the breed, all of which give serious doubts as to what the Colonel claimed. Later in the same year the Earl wrote a letter - of which I have a copy - to the late Elma Stonex, a leading researcher of the breed at the time. The letter is dated "October 26. 52". Three quotes in the letter are of major interest referring to the Colonel and his Russian theory. The Earl writes *"The old man was so convinced that the Caucasian story was correct, that it became a fetish"*. Strong words indeed. Later in the letter he writes - *"Col. Trench has got his dates mixed up!!"* Not the only time! This refers to the dates of the retrievers at Guisachan back in the late 1850's, before Nous arrived and well before the stud book came to light. The Earl goes on to write *"What does surprise me, and I cannot explain it, is his mention of Sandy, as belonging to my father. I certainly can remember no dog by that name in our family"*.

The above gives serious doubt as to what the Colonel was claiming, and this was put in writing by someone who was more than qualified to give his account of the real truth. And what he wrote was confirmed as being the truth, when in 1963 the stud book, so often quoted in this book, and in my previous book (From Yellow to Golden-The Stately Heritage of the Golden Retriever), came to light. It appears that when Dudley Coutts Marjoribanks, the 1st Lord Tweedmouth died in 1894, that it was passed onto his daughter Ishbel - who called the dogs of her father "special yellow retrievers". When she died in 1939 the stud book passed to her daughter, Marjorie, Lady Pentland and when she died in 1970 it was given to the Kennel Club. All this time it was in safe keeping.

For lovers of the Golden Retriever the stud book now remains safe and secure, and anyone who wishes to can see the legacy that Lord Tweedmouth left along with written evidence of how he brought the breed to the canine world.

Presentation page attached by the late Lady Pentland
at the start of the stud book kept by her grandfather,
Dudley Coutts Marjoribanks from 1835 to 1890.

WE WILL NEVER KNOW why the Hon. Colonel William Le Poer Trench pursued his theory that, what we now know as the Golden Retriever, originated from Russia. Perhaps he heard the story that there were once dogs from Russia performing at a circus in Brighton. This was nothing new. At these events in the late 19th century these acts, here and in other places, were common, and often included were a menagerie of animals from across the globe, which, in the 19th century, people would not have seen before and were therefore guaranteed to draw a larger audience.

Also, at this time, the Colonel was aware of what dogs were being bred to work on the land, to assist those whose living depended on having a reliable dog - all day, every day. So why introduce another breed and for what reason? From the time when the journals of the day contained reports of the Colonel and his travels, the dates given were doubtful and further compounded when years later the 6th Earl of Ilchester wrote he had no recollection of his father having a dog called Sandy. Towards the end of his life the records show that the breed he had introduced were not to the liking of others in the dog world, despite their good looks. The dogs he had were known to follow him around his home and estate at St. Hubert's, but then many other breeds would do the same. It should also be remembered that to give instructions that the dogs he had at the time of his death be destroyed, if no suitable home was found for them, does suggest that the breed of dogs which the Colonel brought to the dog world had been a 'failure'.

Despite the fact that the Hon. William Le Poer Trench appears to have discombobulated many in the dog world, I have very much enjoyed the research that I have carried out about him for this book.

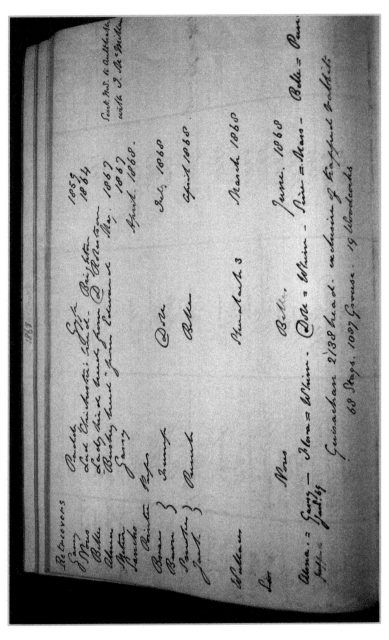

The stud book page for 1868 showing the first entry for Nous - the first Yellow Retriever of many…?

❧ 6 ❧

Renaissance

On the 11th day of November 1918 an agreement was reached by the major countries in Europe to end the First World War which had been fought for over four years. The relief among the nations was shared by all but the effects on people's lives was to remain with them for many months and for some it would never leave them. There were many who hoped and prayed that the bloodshed that had occurred would never be repeated but lessons of warfare are rarely heeded and just two decades later another devastating war would again ruin people's lives.

Prior to the start of WW1 there were many who knew that change was on the way. Many were of the opinion that it would not last long. It was not long before their opinions had to be reconsidered. None of them knew how it would change their lives, but the British character brought a determination from many that they would carry on – regardless! And the dog world certainly played their part as the preceding chapters show. It was not easy. The number of dogs that were registered after 1914 of any breed shows a decline. The reasons for this were obvious. Good homes for puppies born had to be found and breeders were unsure that this would be the case. Money to keep them, both by breeders and new owners, would eat into the domestic budget. Responsible dog lovers were not prepared to run the risk.

The numbers that were registered confirm this. For the Goldens this was 49 in 1914 and by 1917 it had gone down to 7. A year later the figure had gone up to 15. The recovery in litters bred started the following year when 64 were registered and a year later this number was up to 93. The numbers of Goldens recorded do not include those born and sold and whose owners did not choose to have them registered. Despite this I do not believe that the actual number of puppies being born at this time would have been much different. The actual numbers would have shown a decline and then an increase in breeding activity over this time. (I am indebted to the late Frank Weeks for researching the registrations of the Golden Retriever breed during the years quoted).

By 1920 the number of Goldens bred had shown another healthy increase. All that was needed now was somewhere to show them and by the end of this year there must have been celebrations in the dog world when a return of the Crufts dog show in 1921 was announced. The Army had at last vacated the Royal Agricultural Hall in Islington where they had stored equipment to be used in the war and when this was done the dogs could move in, for a few days at least.

The show began on the 2nd February and attracted over 1000 entries - and that was dogs! Of these there were 22 Goldens in 10 classes but it is notable that there was a new group of people exhibiting in the classes from those who had exhibited in the previous Crufts show in 1917.

The person who was to play a major part in showing at Crufts from 1921 to 1930 was the Hon. Mrs Grigg. She had bred a litter out of the Noranby line of Mrs Charlesworth, and they were registered in 1919. She went on to breed her own litters and registered them with the affix Kentford, after the village in Suffolk where she lived. Others nearby saw them, admired them and wanted one or more for themselves and with this the popularity of the breed started to grow once more. Among those who lived nearby and took ownership of these dogs were Mr Braybrook in

The Hon. Mrs Grigg with two of her Golden Retrievers that she bred in 1920.
She was one of the new breeders who assisted the revival of the breed after WW1.

Sudbury, Mrs Evers-Swindell in Saffron Walden, Mr Matthews in Chelmsford, and Mr Rogers in Thaxted. It was not only these places where there was a group of new enthusiasts in a relatively small area at this time. Lady Norton Griffiths, Major Carnegie, Mr W.S. Hunt, and Mr R Hermon all lived in the southern counties of England - Surrey, Hampshire, and Sussex, and when the dogs were old enough would be exhibited at Crufts. By the end of the decade there were 80 Goldens entered for the 25 classes. Many of these would be entered in more than one class. And year on year the numbers increased and would only falter slightly around the time of the next world war.

The background of those who exhibited the dogs during this decade varied. Those whose names I have given were all in the south of England, but, unlike some other breeds, it would be some time before any of the new Golden enthusiasts would travel to London to show at Crufts. No doubt they preferred to support the shows in the more northern parts of the country. Among those who showed their dogs in 1923 were a number of 'ordinary people' - (hope they do not mind me calling them this - it's the dogs which matter) and included Mr G. Lanham, Mr W. Sharratt,

Mrs W. Fletcher, Mrs Potter and Miss E. Charlesworth. This lady was an exception to those who came from the south of England and exhibited their dogs, as she came from Prestbury in Cheshire. I did wonder (as you might) if she was related to 'the' Mrs Charlesworth, but I have not been able to find out if she was.

The dog which she showed was named Butley Bekha and had been bred by a Lady V. Murray. The dog was not placed but if it had been there may have been a problem. The judge for classes of Goldens in 1923 was Mrs Charlesworth (!) and both the dog and bitch of the dogs shown were from the Noranby line of...yes...Mrs Charlesworth herself!

Others who showed in this decade had a military background. They included Captain H.F.H. Hardy, Captain W. Wormald, Lt. Col. Malcolm, Lt.Col. Priorleau and Lt Col. The Hon. D. Carnegie. They not only showed at Crufts, but away from this event they also did credit to the breed by supporting many of the field trial events which had started to take place again.

Another name which should be mentioned at this time is Major Bagnall who in 1921 took over as secretary of the

Golden Retriever Club from Mrs Charlesworth. She had held this position since the formation of the club in 1913. It is more than likely that she decided it was time for a change at the top. Added to this was the fact that she had given extensive service to the Women's Volunteer Reserve during WW1. This had not prevented her having a number of her Goldens with her while working in London. She continued to breed Goldens for many years. Puppies with the affix Noranby in their pedigree would easily find new homes and many of them would be shown at the Crufts show in future years with their new owners. She also kept other Goldens to work with her at field trials which she enjoyed just as much as showing. Mrs Charlesworth also enjoyed days out with a gun, along with other women who took an interest in field trials - and who were often better than the men!

Two events that were to add to the growing popularity of the breed are worth giving as they are connected to the past, and would be for the future. In 1915 a Mr Alfred Higgs was appointed Gamekeeper at Paxhill Park in Sussex, which was owned at that time by William Sturdy. Alfred's father, Edwin, was also a Gamekeeper. It was at

Underley Hall in Westmorland that Alfred was trained by his father. From Paxhill Park Alfred moved to Scadbury Park, Chislehurst, in Kent and it was here that he bred his own Goldens using the affix Scadbury. In the pedigree of his dogs is the affix Noranby.

Major Bagnall on the right, the secretary of the Golden Retriever club from 1921, talking to Commander Holbrook V.C. prior to the start of the Golden Retriever Trials at Godmersham Park which took place in the same year.

Alfred was well known as an expert observer of the temperament and intelligence of the breed, which when the opportunity arose, he would fiercely defend. It was in 'The Gamekeeper' for February 1925 that he took issue with others who said that the breed was "gun shy" and would not get into thick undergrowth. Alfred disputed this and in a polite way told the correspondent that they had been a gun dog for many years and would not have made the progress that they had already as a working dog if they were all actually like that. As to intelligence he cited the occasion when a fellow gamekeeper and his friend were walking with a golden he had bred, along with its two-year-old offspring. The younger dog got into trouble when swimming in a large area of water, treading water but not making any progress. The gamekeeper's friend was about to swim out to it when the older dog pushed them both aside and swam out to the youngster. When it reached its offspring, it pushed him under the water, but seconds later the young dog popped up, grabbed by the ear of his sire and was brought safely back to dry land. Intelligence indeed! This correspondence continued for several weeks, all in favour of the Goldens and is reminiscent of letters which were written to the same journal in the early 1900's. Needless to say the Goldens came out on top - again!

The other event that occurred at this time, and which dog enthusiasts took notice of, was the award of Dual Champion. This is presented to a dog or bitch that is outstanding in the show ring and in the field. In 1921 this was awarded to a Golden by the name of Balcombe Boy.

Dual Golden Retriever Champion Balcombe Boy.

He was born on the 19th March 1919. His pedigree was impeccable coming from the kennel of Lord Harcourt. He had shown his Goldens at Crufts in 1908 and was the first person to show them in the new class for "Retrievers Golden".

Balcombe Boy was owned by Richard Outram Hermon. He was born in 1898 at Staplefield, Sussex. His father, Sidney Albert, had no connections with the dog world, spending much of his life in the cotton industry. Did this pay for what appears to have been a relatively comfortable lifestyle?

In 1911 they lived in The White House in Balcombe, listed as one of the principal properties in Sussex at this time. Also living at this property was Mr W. Hayes who was Richard Hermon's trainer and gamekeeper. Despite the fact that the picture of Mr Hermon shows him dressed for a day's shooting in the field did Mr Hayes deserve just as much credit for getting Balcombe Boy to the level required for him to win the trophy? After this the affix Balcombe would be included in several of the dogs shown at Crufts in the following years.

We know what Balcombe Boy achieved in the dog world but what happened to Mr W. Hayes? That I do not know. Where he came from, what other dogs he trained, where he was born, or died, I have not been able to find out! However, the photo shows he did exist! And with

The owner of Balcombe Boy, Richard Outram Hermon on the right, talking to Capt. Holland during the Horsham and District Retriever Trials in 1921.

*Mr.W.Hayes with Balcombe Boy, trainer and
gamekeeper to Mr Richard Outram Hermon.*

Balcombe Boy he did play his part in bringing the breed to
the attention of the dog world.

In 1930, 563 Golden Retrievers were registered with the
Kennel Club. The breed had recovered from the dark days
of World War One and they would continue to give many
people pleasure in the years to come.

Tailpiece

THE PEOPLE THAT I have written about in this book had one thing in common. They all loved what we now know as the Golden Retriever - and this includes the Hon. Colonel William Le Poer Trench!

When Dudley Coutts Marjoribanks bred the first litter at Guisachan it was the gamekeepers who were quick to recognise the biddable nature of this new working breed, how easy they were to train and the stamina that they had for a long working day. The dogs repeated this day after day. When they finished their working life they would often become a gentle and safe member of a family household.

When any of the keepers chose to take a position on another estate a dog, or two, often went with them. A keeper who was good with a rifle and who had a well-trained dog was always a great asset. Opinions on this new breed would have been passed from keeper to keeper and from estate to estate. Although it was often reported that Dudley never gave any of the bitches away, we do know that this is not correct and without some of them leaving where they were born, we would not have the breed that we have today.

Wherever they went they were admired, their Golden wavy coat proving to be a great attraction. When the coat was smattered with mud after a full day's work retrieving and pleasing its handler, the wonderful smile that said, *"hope you have enjoyed your day as much as I have enjoyed mine"* would have been a picture that would stick in the mind for a very long time.

It was also the gamekeepers who first brought the breed to the show ring in 1901 in reasonable numbers. These shows were run by the Gamekeepers Association. At times this led to controversy with some keepers claiming that the dogs were mongrels. These claims were shrugged off by the Goldens, and their popularity increased year on year.

These shows led onto others for all breeds of retrievers

around the country and included the top show at Crufts and for the Ladies Kennel Association. It was a natural progress for the breed which has now been recognised by the Kennel Club for over 100 years. In that time registrations have increased from 73 in 1913 to 7738 in 2018. The numbers entered at Crufts have also increased and in 2018 over 500 were entered from around this country and from overseas. During this time they have proved to be an extremely adaptable breed.

Although the numbers that are now worked regularly have diminished in favour of other breeds, they are still entered in field trials. They can hold their own at obedience events and at shows. Since the start of this century they have given endless pleasure at events where they are trained for heelwork to music with the public exhibition rings at Crufts being full year after year when they take their place. They are trained to work for several charities, including Medical Detection Dogs, who teach the dog's incredible olfactory sense to recognise when people with specific health issues need alerting to a potentially life-threatening situation.

All the time the breed's character is shown to those around

them, and, unlike some people, they will always do their very best to give kindly satisfaction. They will never turn their back on you or snub you. And when they approach their final days, they will enjoy a comfortable bed and being fed and kept warm and cosy and not be cast aside. Those who do turn them out are not true lovers of the breed. When the awful day comes when one has to make the decision to say goodbye, they will leave you with very happy memories until the day comes when you join them in a better, more tolerant and understanding world.

IS THERE MORE to find about the history of this beautiful breed? The answer is yes - most certainly. New information will come to light, and when it does I hope that those who find it will ensure that it is authentic before they inform others of what they have found. This is the criteria that I have used in this book, and which I also used in the first book; From Yellow to Golden - The Stately Heritage of the Golden Retriever. Only a small part of the research was taken from the internet, which has so much false information. The way to get around this is to go out and meet people who are lovers of the breed and more than willing to talk about the early days and the progress the breed has made, recalling information and memories of friends and relations of the past. In this way I can claim that both books that I have written and published will be a valued addition to the history of the breed. It is my legacy to the breed, indeed a Golden Legacy.

Life's a laugh!

❧ Postscript ❧

A MAJOR SOURCE which has often been referred to is the stud book that was kept by Dudley Coutts Marjoribanks from 1837 to 1890.

It was in 1865 that Nous was first listed and in 1870 when the first 'yellow' puppies were listed.

For 53 years Dudley kept the stud book, often referring to weather conditions and the total number of game 'bagged'. Like most people his handwriting changed over the years but in 1890, the last year that he made an entry, it was still legible. When he died in 1894, the stud book passed to his daughter Ishbel, who often referred to her father's 'special yellow retrievers'. By this time she had married John Sinclair Gordon and they were kept safe in her new home, Haddo House, in Aberdeen-shire. When she passed away in 1939, it was her daughter Marjorie - the future Lady Pentland who was entrusted to keep the stud book safe. Its final journey was in September 1963 when it was given to the Kennel Club and it is here, in the library in safe keeping, for all who would like to see it.

This is less than five miles from where Dudley Coutts Marjoribanks was laid to rest surrounded by many members of his family. Some years ago I was invited to pay a private visit to the burial ground that had been purchased in 1859. After all the research that I had done it was a great

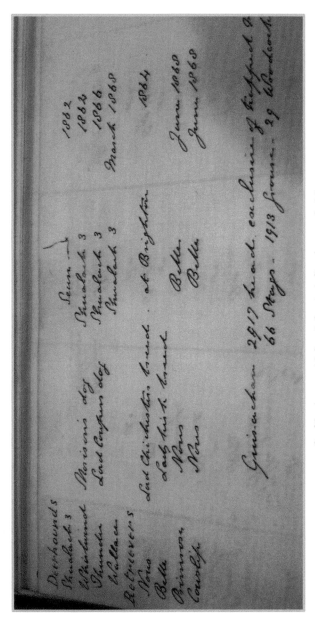

Stud book page with list of dogs including the entry for Nous

133

honour to stand next to his coffin. And yes, on behalf of everyone who loves the Golden Retriever to this day, I did quietly express thanks to him for bringing the breed to the canine world.

He made no response to my thanks. However, on the day of my visit he could have gone to the Kennel Club to check one of his entries in the stud book!

The final resting place.
The author, beside the lead lined coffin of Dudley Coutts Marjoribanks 1820-1894.
His father, Edward 1776-1868, is remembered in the smaller coffin to the left. (Photo from the author's private collection).
Please note: *the family burial grounds are strictly private!*

❧ About the Author ❧

"My interest in this wonderful breed started before my tenth birthday when I spent a holiday with my Uncle who had a small kennel of Golden Retrievers near Poole in Dorset. I was fascinated by their very gentle ways and how they would walk with me through his very large garden. Looking back, they were no doubt also fascinated by me, as at that age I was smaller than they were.

Those memories stayed with me, but it would be many years before circumstances allowed my wife and I to have a Golden of our own: one became two and two became three, such was the attraction of the breed. Our dogs became very much a part of our life and travelled with us on holiday every year. When you have a dog (or two or three) – yes, they all went with us – you always attracted conversation, and it was these conversations that instigated my research into the origins of the breed.

There were a lot of books solely centred on breed lines which I found were not of interest to most people. The people I encountered wanted to know the history of the

"The Goldens of my childhood home."

breed and how they came to the dog world. And when our holidays took us to places where the dogs originated from, it opened up many memories from those who were involved with them in bygone days.

Writing the first book - From Yellow to Golden - The Stately History of the Golden Retriever – brought a gratifying response, with congratulations on the subject which had been thoroughly researched, and not passed down from dubious sources. When additional information came to light, I felt compelled to share this and that's how the sequel - The Golden Era, the Early History of the Golden Retriever - has been written.

Not only did writing these books bring great satisfaction, but also came the reward of being able to support the charity, Medical Detection Dogs. This charity trains dogs of various breeds, including Golden Retrievers, to alert people with serious medical conditions that need to act quickly before things get dangerous. Dogs placed with people in their own homes, not only alert to life threatening situations, but also provide their owners with companionship and security. The charity also works with the dog's incredible olfactory sense to carry out groundbreaking research into the diagnosis of early onset cancers.

Through the sales of the first book, far more than I ever expected, I have subsequently been able to donate money from the sales to this charity, and I aim to continue that support with this book also.

 I consider it an honour and a privilege to be able to support the incredible charity that is Medical Detection Dogs, as well as to have been able to give the background to the development of the equally incredible dog that is - The Golden Retriever."

How to purchase:

From Yellow to Golden - *The Stately Heritage of the Golden Retriever* is available to order from all good bookstores by quoting the following ISBN's:

978 0 9556722 62 *(hardback)*

978 0 9556722 31 *(softback)*

The Golden Era - *The Early History of the Golden Retriever* is also available from all good bookstores

However, if you would like to maximise the amount received by our supported charity (Medical Detection Dogs), please consider ordering a copy (or more!) directly from the author by emailing - malcolm@toadflax.co.uk

Dogs at Carradale, Mull of Kintyre, 1989